AF362081

echoes and mirrors

nero suno

CONTENTS

mirrors

echoes

Echo

Je suis l'amant de moi-même:
the long, longer, longest echo.

Should I become a centenarian

Should I become a centenarian
without counting the stars or the sand,
I should have become myself already
with the stars and the sand in my hands.

I should have become the world in my mind
with a century of conceiving.

Everything I am conceiving is mine,
as I am becoming everything
between the sky and the earth.

        I am time
as long as hundreds of centuries.

Living

Living is not the antithesis of dying,
but of un(loving, hoping & dreaming).
Living
should be how before where & when imagine who.

Trying & failing, either existing in both,
aim for the same what, although which cannot decide
to be chosen or nondecision chooses fate.

(Un)knowing does (not) give up each & every why
with(out) a reason, because finding the right way
is as right as losing the left one, the wrong one
finding & losing itself on its own.

Besides,
being & doing mean more or less needed time
to be & to do till living is been & done.

Becoming a genius

Becoming a genius is here & now
where & when the masterpiece is becoming
infinite & eternal.

Reality
feels more miraculous than mysterious,
because it is real; nothing true is unreal,
even the most unimaginable truth.

Becoming a universe is here & now
where & when the inner peace is perfected.

Space & time are becoming a genius
whose body, mind & soul are a universe.

From adulthood's hour I have been
as others were not; I have seen
as others did not; I can dream
my dreams that are more than they seem.
From midnight to morn I have shaken
my dejection; I have forsaken
my despair heavy as a stone.
And all I live, I live alone.
Now, in my adulthood, before
a most near miracle, I soar
from under with a daring zeal
whose hopefulness is what I feel
from the torrent, or the fountain,
from the red cliff of the mountain,
from the sun above the world
in its summer tint of gold,
from the lightning in the sky
touching my wings as I fly,
from the thunder, and the storm
and the cloud that takes the form
(when Heaven celebrates my youth)
of the spirit of my truth.

The world hides no more secrets from me

The world hides no more secrets from me.
It has found new hopes and dreams to fool.
Hoping in dreams was what I fooled best;
dreaming in hopes is what I fool worst.

The world used to hide secrets from me
when I had songs to sing. I used to
dance when the world was watching. I had
hopes and dreams that the world fooled, always.

Everything has changed yet nothing has.
The world has changed me yet it has not.
I still have songs to sing and I dance
even though the world is not watching.

Like a ghost

Like a ghost, I'm not like a host at all.

I'm a lone ghost dancing in my own ball
among unwanted guests who see me through.
These uninvited guests invite more fools
queueing in a mess outside my castle.

By their joy, my grief's reduced to rubble.

The music plays on with my tragedy
ridiculing aloud my travesty.
Half drunk wine spills foolishness in the air
where it smells of craziness everywhere.

Like a ghost, I'm weightless and powerless.
I'm a lone ghost, as hopeless as helpless.

In melancholy I was born to die.
I don't crave any much more or less life
that these unthankful guests impose on me.

Ghostly, merely in my mind I exist.

I am first and foremost an animal

15

I am first and foremost an animal
however I dream to be whatever
I live to be. Thanks to hunger and thirst,
I live to be an animal only.

Being an animal should be enough,
if hunger and thirst are never too much.
Being what I am is never enough.
I am forever hungry and thirsty.

The present, the future and the past

The present
is living in me,
                    the end of the world
living in the future.
                        Every day is wonderful
and I am thankful.
                    Otherwise,
how else can I be and what can I do
if every day is dreadful?

I am thankful for the past
that was both wonderful and dreadful.

But why is the future living in me
when every day can be the end of the world?

Because
the past is living in me
and because
the world did not end.

My biggest talent

My biggest talent is to appreciate
the absolute good in humanity.
This is a talent (out of which I am
making a genius) I was born without.

Wherever I go, I see beauty only.
Beauty is what I feel, hear, touch and taste.
Everybody inspires (my every sense
to become) the best artist in me. At least,

(being overconfident,) I stay inspired
when humanity tries to fail itself
throughout history. At most, nothing lasts
before a genius with nothing to prove.

My second biggest talent is to forget
the absolute good in humanity.

Our love

Our love, my most felt creation
& your most known abstraction,
is our most felt & known perfection.

I feeling you & you knowing me,
our love doesn't need translation
or want interpretation between us.

Our love is poetry writing itself.

As poetry, our love is made
everywhere in the world, right here,
whenever we are one, forever.

Right here & forever
our love feels & knows perfection.

Love is in the moment

Love is in the moment, so is every
(illimitably imagining) thing
else (breathing, growing and imagining
how to realise a dream to marry)

that is changing the (solitary) world
(irrevocably grows the universe)
by (irrevocably) changing themselves
(no love is irrevocably returned).

Will we love each (kiss) other more or less
in the next moment, (in the last moment
we were breathing, remembering a stone
carrying the weight of the universe)

or (surely) not at all, since (love began)
we love each (kiss) other perfectly (true)
in this very moment (our love is new
(old being easier to understand))

where the world and every (imagining)
thing in it (entirely love) are changing?

This is not love, they say

25

This is not love, they say.
                    They know
what they know.
                    What I have to say
is
   I know how my body feels
itself and life with your body.

How my mind minds mindfully
our skins, bones, hair and muscles
was unknown to me till now.

I wonder what else is there to know
if all I need is forever now
knowing my body better than
it feels itself and life with you.

Maybe this is not love as they say.

But yes, life and I love each other
while you are right in between.

kisses impregnate

27

kisses impregnate, didn't you know?

now you must know that our kisses
impregnate a song with a voice
(every living thing carries one),
because every living thing hears
the joy singing in our bodies.

now when our tongues touch our spirits
(more touchable than by our hands),
the dead appear to come alive.

our kisses bring spring to the dead,
the cold and the hopelessly sad
(hopefully, our gladness feels life).

now until forever let's kiss
the world, it's so gracious to us.

Our making love is a fine genius

29

Our making love is a fine genius
making music merely for himself.
It is a myth in a miracle.
We are two miraculous genii

made out of love. This mythical love
holds all the answers, but does not tell.
How rich! Our music is made to feel
our bodies in each other among

numberless possibilities. Time
desires eternity, space as well.
Dreams sound as musical as hopeful.
Life is perfectly lived in our prime.

Next to love, sex

Next to love, sex is the best thing in life
without any doubt of hunger or thirst.
Hence, I eat all your sex after drinking
all your love, both being life at its best.

How I am greedy and how you are rich
in what I need! To survive every day,
I need what I want from your love and sex.
To survive every night, you possess me
more than I possess my vitality.

Sex is the best thing in life next to love
when you love me sexually. Only
your soul should master my body truly
and I let your body master my soul.

With the promise of the best things in life,
we are better and better together.

We are loving and sexing forever.

By swallowing you as a whole

By swallowing you as a whole,
I feel my hunger and thirst grow
(on behalf of all humanity
that is craving for love) silently

into a rapacious monster
in my belly.
           Such a monster
(on behalf of all monstrosities)
grows back into all humanity
every time I feel full and quenched.

If love has to feel full and quenched,
no love is to blame for this
monstrous metamorphosis.

satiety is insatiable

satiety is insatiable
because it feeds itself

i do not care
if you should doubt
the intention of the world
is to destroy
rather than make and mend
while november is feeling warm
with us lying in bed

our sex grow
more intelligent than our brains:
renounce all thoughts
that intend to destroy

feel november against our skins

satiety feeds itself
because it is insatiable

TAO

THE WAY i am
instantly after
ejaculation
:
i am THE WAY

Dildodils

I cruised aimlessly as a cloud
that floats on high o'er males and thrills,
when queerly I noticed a crowd,
a troop of XL dildodils;
beside the snakes, behind the beasts,
standing hard in the wilderness.

Lascivious as mouths that bite
and dribble in a hungry way,
they poked with neverending rhymes
along the swaying music play:
ten thousand stroked I all at once,
still craving more in lustful trance.

The cave beside them roared; but they
out did the growling cave in spree:
a poet could not but be gay,
in such a spermy company:
I sucked and sucked, but little thought
what meal the flesh to me had brought:

Very oft, when alone I lie
in cool or in erotic mood,
they echo on that inward cry
which is heaven among nude dudes;
and then in my heart gay I feel,
and dream about the dildodils.

If my life is wasted

If my life is wasted, what about yours?

Are you sadly happy on my behalf
or happily sad like everyone else
who wastes at least something in his(her) life?

Since everything in life can be wasted,
my life and yours can be simply exchanged,
so can be yours and everyone else's.

But what does "waste" mean among meaningless
beings and doings in life?
                              Meaningful
beings and doings in life waste the same
law of nature between an animal
and a human, both of which are wasteful.

If my life is wasted, much more is yours.
And I refuse to exchange yours with mine.

Meal

43

Knowing my meal tastes the same in your mouth,
I lose appetite. And I feel sorry
for the meals tasting the same in all mouths.
Am I being dumb? I am not worried.

My tongue tastes what a tongue could imagine
or would rather not. I am voracious
because life is generous. Imagine
a life with only one taste! Infamous!

Bitterness, the most raw ingredient,
tastes most true, tasteful sourness coming next.
Spiciness, the reddest ingredient,
flavors other tasteless colors as well.

Sweetness is added much more than needed
wherever water should suffice and wine
drinks itself. No appetite is needed
whenever your meal tastes the same as mine.

What else can you do?

Dislike me, pls.
                Despise me in spite of
your spice of life being tasteless fast food,
my life being each healthy ingredient.

Detest me, although I'm wrongly tested
neither positive nor negative, still
you're almost a victim accurately.

Hate me!
        Hate me!
                Hate me with all your hate
that you know now you're able to let out!

Curse the beauty before my eyes.
                          I hear
music whenever I see ugliness.

My apology for your annoyance
won't be accepted.

                Curse, no matter how
impossibly I'm unaffected.
                Curse
until your last breath giving force to mine.

Satisfy my needs, don't disappoint me.

What else can you do? I'm so curious.

now I realise

47

now I realise
              (until now I didn't realise)
I lack a friend,
              I feel (sadly
I'm not a lacking friend)
more than ok which is also ok.

I used to use my friends
who used me friendly
with life being forever unfriendly.

all friends use one another altogether
against life.

to be useful is why a friend lacks a friend.

now I realise I'm useless, I feel
free which is more than lonely.

Emptiness is felt enough

49

Emptiness is felt enough to be real.
It is seen,
          heard
               and stroked,
                         being filled with
everything that can be filled with until
fullness is felt enough to be unreal.

The emptiness in me sees,
                    hears
                         and strokes
the emptiness all around me,
                    feeling
the fullness in me that feels real until
the fullness all around me feels unreal.

At this very moment

51

At this very moment, as I'm unknown
to someone who (I'll never get to know)
is fleeing a war or lucky enough
to create one, I have nothing to lose

or gain in my own world where I'm at peace.
And I don't depreciate either truth
as long as I'm happy with my own lie:
I need nothing more or less till I die.

At this very moment, as I become
someone unknown who (I already am)
is dying in bed or living somewhere
before dying there, I'm dying to leave

and never return unless the whole world
gives a damn about everyone's own world.

Suicide

Suicide isn't a matter of free will
(whether I was willing to be born was),
though I'm willing to die, or so I feel.
And I feel I'm willing to live as well

when suicide is a matter of time.

Surviver

Except courage, life has left me nothing
(have I had everything?) more cowardly.

To survive is a coward's specialty.

I am courageous enough to survive
this & next beyond mediocrity
(between five to nine) after nine to five.

I am thankful enough to be lucky
(between nine to five) after five to nine
when life takes something away from someone.

No one has had everything that life gives,
even the most courageous surviver.

I am a mediocre surviver.

psychopath

57

a self made psychopath makes himself
at home among families of members
feeling christmas in the air. christmas trees
beautify other trees in the cities
and forests no less. even the deserts
celebrate, wishing for snow that doesn't melt.

he remembers how to be natural
like the snow that won't fall in the deserts,
because he was a christmas tree standing
somewhere in the distance. it was freezing
outside until inside he was frozen.
he forgets how to be unnatural.

he'll be a self destructive psychopath
alone in the deserts of australia
next christmas. it'll be in summer with rain.
then, he'll be no longer a psychopath.

a stranger

a stranger
different
from
(everyone's hungry neighbour

could would should

WISH for
the next war
happening already
in a rich neighbourhood)

none other than
myself

(i was hungry once or twice
when three or more strangers)

walked by.

At the corner of falling in love

At the corner of falling in love
& out of, I find & lose myself
in every way spontaneously.

Simultaneously, somebody
is all ready to be found & lost
by love waiting to be fallen in
& out of.

    & I & somebody
fall into each other entirely
at this very corner, in a crowd
finding & losing love randomly,
before we fall out of each other
partly, returning into the crowd.

Out of the craziest craziness

Out of the craziest craziness, you
come to be in my head and there you stay.
You are perfect because I am crazy.
I know that I am crazy, yes, I know.

Nothing compares to your perfect body
but your perfect love. Your body and love
that belong to me only are beyond
comparison to everything that dreams.

I could even endure hunger and thirst
with you in my head. I could even face
the world that is as crazy as I am.
However, I would sooner close my eyes
and SEX with you till this crazy world ends.

Crush

You make me feel like a natural poet,
for when I look at the sky, I see your face.
And when I look at your face, I see myself
fall in love with the whole world.

                             It's a poem
for you, my new love, my yet to be true love.

I wake up in the morning still dreaming of
you. I'm dreaming of us dancing in the crowd.
I'm a dreamer, but don't let me dream alone.

Will you follow me to the place unknown? Or,
I'll follow you if you know where we're going.
Will you allow me to love you as I love
everything lovable? Well, you can love me
however you want to.

                    When & wherever
we're together, we'll be closer & closer;
where & whenever we're apart, in our hearts,
we're together. My dear, do you love me yet?

sex me, love me, marry me or kill me

sex me, love me, marry me or kill me,
these are the only ways you should do me
(the only ways to save me from this life,
too real for fantasies to feel alive).

sex me as you need not learn how to love,
because i feel your love when you believe.
marry me if you dare give up this world
(much better at killing than believing).

this world will kill itself by killing all.

before all, all has been done, after all.

sex me, love me, marry me and save me,
these are the only ways i should be killed.

You conquer me

69

You conquer me through carelessness among
other heartlessness, because I let you.
I let myself be lovable to you,
as well. I fail. Unless I let the sun

always shine on beauty only, my life
has to find beauty on its own. (I am
beautiful when I am loved; I am more
beautiful when I am conquered by love.)

Now that I am conquered by lovelessness,
I do not let you make me or my life
less beautiful than you and your life. Why
does not the sun shine on beauty only?

Slowfinally

Slowfinally, the night opens its thighs
for the day when electrons and nerves make
all openness wide enough for the ride.

Wider than the night staying wide awake,
the day measures its pleasure against space.

No wonder truth ridicules science.

Breathe
and find the world some freedom in each breath.

Mouth to tongue, the nearest distance comes close
until tongue to throat, a heart finds the world.

Science understands truth in this wonder.

I love you, because

I love you, because you don't love me back
the way everything begins and ends.

Either both of us know what love is,
or neither of us know how to love.

You don't love me back, because I love you,
(not) knowing everything begun, ends.

Either both of us know how to love,
or neither of us know what love is.

Determination

I'm determined to have talent
in everything I do, therefore
I imagine me being loved
by you when I've nothing to do.

To appreciate life can be
waited, to fear of death as well.
Time stops creating and killing
before you do love me, my love.

I don't have to do anything
because I'm talented to love
the way I imagine. I'm sure
time will create and kill once more.

I have to believe

I have to believe that I loved you,
because the world ever feels the same
love in joyful pain and painful joy
(not because my life is not the same
life in painful pain and nothing else),
without me loving you anymore.

I am sure that I do not love you
anymore and I almost cannot
believe that the world still feels the same
pain and joy, my life being the same.

Immorally

Immorally, I have solely
one purpose to serve as a slave:
to be someone else's master
(you, my love, being my master)
in love and to destroy this love
before his very eyes, only
to feel firstly, how you should feel
breaking my heart, body and soul,
secondly, how you should not feel
as if you would be the master
forever, thirdly, how you fail,
how you fail, how you fail to love.

Rome

Rome was not built in one day,
but ruined in one sec.
A built-to-be-ruined city it was
where all lives lived and all deaths died.

What one could see elsewhere was heard there;
what one could hear there was seen elsewhere.
A common city it was.
No one from elsewhere had to go there.

No one had to build it
and no one would have to ruin it soon after.
However,
no one seems to forget it,
everyone seeing and hearing the same thing everywhere.

Everyone lives and dies the same way everywhere.

HEAVEN knows

83

HEAVEN knows how each&every god
fucks to be fucked common sense, because
HELL doesn't know how to give rein to us
who fuck to be fucked nonsense of course.

HELL needs little doubt in the devil
trying his best to rival a fool.

HELL can't even burn out of itself
with the bones too dry to crack open
the same old world with the flesh so soft.

We eat each other as long as there's hope
and nothing not yet born tastes better
than the happiness of another.

We puke right before HEAVEN&HELL
turn upside down.
                GENESIS is sealed.

I was born yesterday

I was born yesterday
and so were you.
We were
lost and found at the same place too.

I am alive today
and so are you.
We are
close enough to be more than two.

I will die tomorrow
and so will you.
We will
kill each other if we have to.

jeune et jolie

jeune et joli parce que je suis
i speak french that i don't mean
i mean whatever that i don't speak
before the keen world before me

you'll never see what i've seen
before the keen world before me
i'm enough crazy and most lonely
a friend isn't worth two enemies

i don't mean what i do speak
vieux et moche quand meme je suis
something owes me my goodness
the world is keen before me

my badness owes me nothing
avant tout le monde je m'excuse
i'm keen before a lover or two
an enemy is worth two or more friends

before the keen world before a lover
i misunderstand myself after all
i've seen the world and i'll be a lover
quand meme je suis jeune et joli

peace is harder to understand than war
war being harder than love
before the keen world before me
mais quoi que ce soit je m'en fiche

Imagination is the will of boredom

Imagination is the will of boredom.
No wonder I am imaginatively
bored when I have the will to be an artist.

But I do wonder if I am an autist
with enough noises and voices around me.

The world is sick, boredom being one symptom,
lovelessness the other. These two will suffice
the excuse of all unimaginative
unhappiness.
            Hence, I have the will to be
everything the world is against, simply
something more imagined than ordinary.

I lose my happiness as a sacrifice.

Gamble on the weather

Gamble on the weather being
however it will be and do
whatever you have to do.

                        Who
should feel so unlucky to win
the rain or luckier to lose
the scorching sun in summer?

In spite of the perfect weather
having nothing to win or lose,
you cannot prepare for the end
of the game that life is playing.

Life plays with everyone's luck, since
everyone's life on luck depends.

Life is the essential meaning
of gambling, weather permitting.

November

November is a failed disaster.
Congratulations to all other
disasterous failures in a year.

Life is failing itself to become
death. Nevermind, neither is enough
personal, both being what they are.

I remember my future as this:
someone lost her future more than his
when someone else forgot how to lose.

If only the sky knew how to choose
today among the days already
chosen, destiny should be ready
to fulfill one's dreams that are empty.

Monthly, the sky knows nothing but rain
in this time of year raining in vain.

Before an imminent catastrophe

Before an imminent catastrophe,
a tide of desperate euphoria
washes over me. Such a fantasy!
What happens next? I have no idea.

Should I be drowned, let me sink deep and low
to the bottom of humanity. Or,
let the water clean everything once and
for all, everything burnt down to the ground.

Should I be saved, prepare me for the worst
that is yet to come. Sooner or later,
history must be redeemed from itself.
The worst will always return as the best.

After a brand new catastrophe,
my world lives in a better fantasy.

Life is not bad at all

Life is not bad at all, I am not dead.

Thanks to my mother's love, the only love
my love should return to, I am not dead.

Standing on the slope of Vesuvius,
I envisage my fall in daring mood,
for I have not fallen and I will not.

Life is not bad at all under the moon.
It is dark, but I have seen the daylight.
And I shall see the sun rise tomorrow
with my mother's love keeping me alive.

I was ready to die ages ago
and when I aged old enough, I chose life.

Life is not bad at all, I am content
to live dangerously with death in mind.

Before destiny, I rule and possess.

Life tastes still better than death in my mouth.

Blue

99

Strawberries are blue.

This is how my life
is incredibly true
:
I have not changed at all
since strawberries turned blue,
not since blueberries grew.

Until blue is the mere color
under the sky,
with blackberries being untrue,
nothing credible will change me.

mirrors

Mirror

Living in the mirror on one's wall,
I lose count of my recurring life.

Appointment

NAIVETE and JUVENILE and ADULTHOOD
have an appointment somewhere in time.
                                    sooner
forgotten than remembered, all three grow old,
missing one another patiently later.

most disenchanted, NAIVETE stays naive
on behalf of ADULTHOOD who departs first.
forever lost in every way, JUVENILE
misunderstands every perspective reversed.

I behold and take heed in the near distance
when in the far nearness I am unconcerned.

my life is young enough to experience
what happens next until SENIOR reappears
out of nowhere in time with no appointment.

that memory does not betray this moment.

Reverie

105

i woke up this morning, speaking the truths
(that no one comprehends in a language)
about untruths from A to Z.
                                        how strange!
how can a Bee be unafraid of death,
when a fish either eats or gets eaten
in the C?
                in D, i am so defiled
in the East that i feel very much Free.

Geesus saved from Hell, an eye for an I.
Jesus fell from heaven, total Karma.

Laugh, since all is absurd. Without music,
all is Nonsense. Oh, Please, stand in the Q,
although your blood Runs faster than a Snake.

and time is needed to make the best Tea
for U, the Vip in black and White,
Xcept that because does not question Y.

the truths well deserved, i go back to sleep.

I am the mere smart one here

I am the mere smart one here, with one eye
seeing and the other one believing
I am the mere smart one here.
                          With one ear
hearing and the other one believing
I am the mere smart one here, my body
is locked. My body locks all my smartness
inside and no more smartness could break in.

I stay here, because everywhere I go
is just the same. I am the mere smart one
wherever I am, with my brain working
the way merely I could see and hear things
that make me believe things that I believe.

Zoom!

Zoom!
       Show the world what your eyes wish to see.

Show each&everywho within yourself
how a flower consummates the summer
in the white heat inflaming the windstorm.

Show tomorrow today's sunrise&set
against the silhouette of yesterday.

As far as the sky doesn't fall, the ground calls
our ears hearing the world in all wishes.

Starting a new life
is an old idea
before death
when neither life nor death changes.

Ideally,
newness and oldness exchange
as long as days
are as short as nights,
really,
ending something
is as difficult as
starting everything.

As impossible as being nothing,
life is neither new nor old
still
after death.

My father was disappointed in me

My father was disappointed in me,
so is my mother, all because
I am disappointed in life.
What life let them be, I will not do;
what life let me be is disappointing.
I will be disappointing
until life is not.

My mother is disappointed in life,
so was my father, however,
I am not disappointed in them.

I am not disappointed in myself.

I will not let life be what it has always done.

Optimism

Optimism can never have enough of
what an optimist does not need.
       This world
has enough of its optimistic fools
until it needs more.
      And I wonder why
everybody envies wisdom, sort of.

Wisdom is not always enviable,
no wonder a fool is still wonderful.

Pessimism is much easier, maybe.

Unhappiness

Unhappiness is worth nothing
other than itself. Nonetheless,
it lives to kill everything else
till nothing else is left to die.
In vain, everything is dying
on its own already. In vain,
the world was born to live and die.
Nothing worthy of happiness
lives on forever when the world
is worthy of unhappiness.
In vain, I was born in this world
unhappily to be happy.

when machines need to compose poetry

when machines need to compose poetry
and wars fall short of legal massacres,
when orgasms spawn outside of a palm tree
and canon in d bombs mediocre

when snow freezes in color red and pink
in june, winter disregards monochrome
and solitude outlives much love and like
or else a skyscraper builds down each tomb

when religions cease to produce nonsense
against comics, dinosaurs are served as
lunch in an asian household and a fence
awaits to restore confidence with ease

i still won't disbelieve in that moral
high ground of mankind (over animals)

Obsessed, I surrender

Obsessed, I surrender.
                    Disenchant me
(certainly not the first time but the last)
or proffer me a miracle. There's no
miracle.
            There's no miracle.
                            There's no
other way to exit this urgency.

There's not a single miracle at all.

I'm burning in water and drowned in fire.
Strangely, I'm feeling more alive than dead.

I'm certian of any uncertainty
life is proud of.
                Gone is my pride.
                            I'm weak
as I've never been. I'm getting weaker
until exhaustively I surrender.

Your disbelief

Your disbelief deserves nothing true.

My love was among everything true
you disbelieved, ergo, you did not
deserve it and it is becoming
untrue.

      Each day, I accelerate
the process, because I hate my love
being neither true nor untrue.

                    Love
should be forever celebrated
by the truth it bequeaths the loved one.

The truth is love for the loving one.

Now that my love has become untrue,
your belief deserves all the untruths
dying to love the way I loved you.

The truth is, I will never love you.

nothing closer to love is hate

125

nothing closer to love is hate
close enough to unfeel the same
contrariety on a face
forgotten how to immitate
life in disguise of death
                        it takes
more than a killing to repay
the failed romance if heartbreaks may
or may not repair themselves
                              shame

love begins to end
                    and in hate
time finds all lost patience to save
the rest of what cannot be saved
when love ever comes before hate
far enough to feel the same love

nothing farther to hate is love

What's wrong with me if

What's wrong with me if nothing's right with you?
We'd find someone (or something) else to blame.
There're enough of them between me and you,
between wrong and right, between blame and blame.

Between no and yes, the world has to choose,
even if there were more choices elsewhere.
Between war and peace, there's no place for truth,
even if there were, truth wouldn't lie to stay there.

Between death and life, luck (called destiny)
predetermines all between time and space
where you find heaven in hell to blame me.
I find hell in heaven in you. Disgrace!

Between hate and love, we have to survive
and learn from every blame that'll survive us.

Love is political

Love is political.
    Love makes less sense
than two politicians talking nonsense.
Love is a game of power as long as
it fears of both truths and lies that itself
tells.
  The basic law of the universe
is misunderstood by politicians
(in politics, there are only losers),
because love is not to be understood.

Love is political enough to be
hypocritical when it is stupid
enough to be absolute. When it is
smart enough to be what it claims to be,
one can be politically in love.

And I am a politician in love.

My love is dangerous

My love is dangerous, because I am
dangerous. Safely, life is not sorry,
having made me the way my love is true,
nonetheless.

I am dangerously true.

No one wants to be loved by me, unless
his love is more dangerous than my hate
whereof I myself am mostly fearful.

My hate is dangerously as true as
my love.

I am not fearful of someone
dangerous if he does love me truly.
If he does not love me dangerously,
his hate will be thankful for mine one day.

My love and hate are not sorry for me,
nor am I sorry for life and its truth.

Your body's been to the end of the world

Your body's been to the end of the world,
your mind with someone else in is still there.

Your heart cannot decide as usual,
wanting more than a heart can feel.

                                  Somewhere
in the middle is where you built your house
whose very last host you said I must be.

I've been gazing way too far in the haze.

Someone else differently same as me
is moving in from the end of the world,
patiently as soon as I'll be homeless.

My body's leaving for another world,
my mind with you in is still in your house.

My heart cannot decide, but it has to.
It wants only so much to feel for you.

Doubt

135

Doubt, tell me where he is with whom now.
Tell me what they are doing and how.
Tell me if his mind feels as happy
as his body feels brand new. Tell me
everything I refuse to believe,
although it is fine to be naive.
And say no if yes is the answer,
because I will not question either.

Doubt, was he ever in love with me
or is he still in love with himself?
Doubt, will he ever come back to me
or should I learn to love myself? Well,
doubtlessly, Doubt, you have no idea.

Doubtlessly, Doubt, I have no idea.

Betrayal

Betrayal always does a perfect job
in the name of a fool who deserves it.

I am a betrayal deserving fool,
because I thought love deserved to be me
(when love was already everything else
that made me fall in love with you).

Gravely, it was not in love where I fell,
(when I thought you fell in love with me too)
but in betrayal where I think I will
never get out of without being loved
by you.
        A fool will always be a fool
and you will always betray me unless
you will be betrayed sooner or later
by the love that you will always deserve.

Vengeance

Vengeance knows its way home, having
both of our life the rest of.

Hate
will guide it through forgetfulness
when goodness deigns to be weakness;
pain will retain guilt, crime and shame
where religion must always fail.

Along the way, in sacrifice,
beauty concedes the world's ugliness
with art prefering tragedy.

Appreciate the color blood
running from your eyes drowned in tears.

I shall witness your final fears
as I was victim of your all...

Should fate try its folly once more,
we should perish right before love.

We did love each other.
Or not?

A stupid child

A stupid child with an innocent air
hopes nothing for humanity,
                            because
nothing is to be hoped for in human
ity whose most innocent masterpiece
is a stupid child growing up faster
than all the stupidity in the world.

Vice versa,

Much too smart inhumanity requires
no innocence from a smart child,
                                because
a grown up is smart enough to make peace
with himself and the world where inhuman
ity destroys everything hopefully
hoping hopes are safe with the dead only.

Pure evil never needs an excuse

143

Pure evil never needs an excuse
for pure stupidity,
even if it's evil enough to be smart.

Even if it's stupid enough to be good,
impure evil
serves as an excuse
for impure smartness.

Impure stupidity aiming to be pure smartness,
serves not only as the only excuse
for impure evil,
but also
the only excuse
for impure good.

Pure good never needs an excuse for itself.

Imagine that money is everything

Imagine that money is everything,
everything that you can imagine.

Imagine that sex is money
and love is neither saved nor spent.
Imagine that faith is money
in a faithless world full of faces.
Imagine that art is money
when beauty is not worth a penny.
Imagine that power is money
buying everything powerless.
Imagine that fame is money,
anonymity as well.
Imagine that you are money,
your actions and words, your body and soul.

Just imagine
with all the money that you have.

Imagine harder
with all the money that you can imagine to have.

Laziness is a fathermucker

Laziness is a fathermucker
and I am a prince.
                    I am lazy
in the new days growing old, new days
that count numbers when a prince grows old.

I am busy once in a blue moon,
twice in a green sun, three and more times
in a colorless sky.
                    As a prince
of a kingdom of fathermuckers,
I do whatever I do not do
as long as new days are yet to come.

Except that sleep is never tired of
its dreams, even for a lazy prince.

I hate hunting

I hate hunting as much as Hemingway
loved it in his earnest, literally.
Why is it always either love or hate?
Because either I kill or you get killed.

I hate hunting. I should prefer killing
human beings, if I deserved enough
money & time. If I procured a gun,
I should prefer killing human beings.

I should deserve enough money & time,
if my masculinity defined me.
In good earnest, Hemingway loved hunting;
in bad earnest, hunting killed Hemingway.

If, among all choices, I had a choice
which I do not have, (un)fortunately,
I should prefer killing human beings.
I should even eat those I should have killed.

I should even eat those I should have killed,
if I was hungry for human nature.
I am not hungry for human nature.
It makes me sick, in good & bad earnest.

how adjectively!

how adjectively!

how adjectively! would subjunctive mood unbe me
after the possessive determiners,
who, despite every gone and given,
do formal imperatives in favour of argumentatives anyway?

moreover, which verb predicates me to be perfect
amongst simple present tenses
by means of negation-cum-comparison?

if it weren't for an upside-down arrow,
opposite pronouns( ) can save pronounciations
between adverbs and proverbs à la entre guillemets
respecting a portmanteau vis-à-vis a semicolon,
since abroad equals overseas in view of elsewhere.

nonetheless, as per angle a parellel degree,
nevertheless is more than forever in addition to nowadays,
meantime with somewhat reference to objects
on account of extra paragraphs minus stanzas.

apostrophe is not needed for what is mine( ),
while counting infinity is...

thanks to the best sentence( ) bar none,
I am notwithstanding atop indeed,
concerning astride all other subjects underneath.

This poem vowed to praise love

This poem vowed to praise love (something
it did, does or will not believe in
among alphabets and their reverse)
only to glorify sex (something
it did, does or will not have enough
between night and bed).

                    This poem vowed
to mean literally what someone
understands, only to doubt itself
before someone misunderstands all
in terms of love and sex.

                    This poem
vowed to save the world, only to die
silently without much love or sex.

virginity masturbates

virginity masturbates
                    let it
destroy what must be ruined today

tomorrow stays unfinished business
which is no one else's but nonsense

both married and divorced fantasies
misunderstand life
                    death understood

now molest organic potence
before an impotent orgasm
after an orgy
              would rather fake

condoms kill more abortions will rape
more profane saints than mundane perverts

a penis cannot grow introvert

a pussy can only grow softer
in the name of all fucked honesty

Any pussy finds home in a princess

Any pussy finds home in a princess.
Opps, cunt is the word I can never say
(alas, cunt is the word I did say twice),
except when a bitch gets lucky.

                            Incest
is made out of the handsomely rich prince
(rich on behalf of the entire country)
who has a taste for foreign fruits, I guess.
A lusty prince fucks a slutty princess.

Together, they build a house in the news,
otherwise, what should they undo like us?
Unlike us, they are born to live then die
in the making-the-world-go-square limelight.

Somebody has to win the lottery,
the rest being happy to celebrate.
A loser is proud of his(her)story.
Every day zombies go on a parade.

The dying woman

159

The dying woman, ghastly in her bones,
When young people die, she would sigh for them;
When she wriggles within more sheets than one:
The stink a dark coffin cannot contain!
Her ugliness only ghosts should reveal,
Or Nordic men who fall ill in the heat
(I'd have them vomit as one, shriek to shriek).

Oh, her prime's long gone! She strokes that gray chin,
She tries to turn, and counter-turn, and grunt;
She tries to touch, my youthful asian skin;
I startle unruly from her worn hand;
She's deadly sick; I, poor I, the great pain,
Sitting beside her for her dying sake
(But what tiresome caring we two do fake).

Hate loves a slander, and adores a goon:
Her lips slackened, the gasping choke to ease;
She slays it quick, she slays it for fruit juice;
My eyes, they appall at her twisting feet;
Her single fart could kill a purple rose,
Or a burning fever with a stuffed nose
(She fools the turtles, and those turtles fool).

Let meat be ass, and ass be on display:
I'm hero to an emotion I own;
What's karma for? To know oblivion.
I swear she casts a spell toxic as coal.
But who would count oblivion in days?
These old bones die of their unwanted ways:
(I fear death by how a body decays).

...and morning is a better lover than

161

...and morning wakes a better lover than
dreams sleep best in their infidelity.

all that is early is open and free.
time punishes all that is late, although
love fails to wait for itself before now
(love is forever waited less and less).

...but morning wakes someone in love alone
or twice as much, as much as old is new
(love favors new until dreams are no more
something that everyone is hopeful for).

...and morning wakes a lover full of dreams.
...but morning wakes a dream without lovers.

when the bird abandons the sky

when the bird abandons the sky,
feel for the sky that drops its height.
in contempt of the ocean's tears,
the wind's dream awakes and cries.

should years regret the sky in time,
wait till the ocean drowns and dries.
the wind stops to hear a prayer,
"let the bird forget how to fly."

the ocean breathes out the clouds' forlife,
the wind grieves, "bliss is never mine."
freedom hides away from the bird,
thus the sky hangs low with a sigh.

the wind blows still, questioning "why?"
a skyless bird sings too much pride.
a birdless sky needs no more songs
if on the ocean no light shines.

An amaranthine flower

My flower is ephemeral and
I shall not stay much longer either.

I shall water it (already gone
by summer) until deep autumn and
I shall depart before the first snow.

I shall not stay where memories cry
(memories cry because they die) and
winter refuses to welcome spring.

An amaranthine flower will bloom
where all four seasons remember me.

You are a tree and how silly of me
to try to make you feel more than a tree!

You do feel the earth, the sun and the wind,
but not a silly bird's craving, a bird
singing for the sake of being alone.

With a singing bird, a tree is alone.

A tree is not a bird's mere destiny.
Withal, a lonely bird craves company.

Why are we together, if both lonely?
We are together so both less lonely.

The ending

The ending is there waiting.
I can see it already
if you feel it in the wind.

The ending is waiting there,
not going anywhere, unlike us.
The ending is where we are heading.

Let us not hurry or worry
even though the sky is raining.
Our journey began in the rain
as I remember perfectly.

Imperfectly, let us forget
our journey in the rain and wind.

Hopefully the day will be sunny
when we arrive eventually.

true love

171

still i don't wonder true love exists
after doubting if it doesn't exist
in all corners of my mind or whose,
because a foot belongs to more shoes

with zero excuse of untrue love,
a million unwishes from above
jinx a billion fools running bare foot
on the road filled with worn out shoes

why does everything in existence
seem eitheror untrue in a mind
& why does not everyone in love
declare his true foot fetish in shoes?

to be true is more false than to love

to be true is more false than to love,
thus i try harder than the world fails.
i am tired till i shall not give up
overthinking lastly before first.

i am tired doing what i must think
being being loved like a false truth,
although i can try any harder
than the world fails to be loved, or not.

were i anything but a lover
of something lovable, i must be
everything true till the world is still
more if than yes with countless heartaches.

to fulfill all changeable wishes,
i search and find all wishful changes
more then than now wherever i lay.
with too many dreams, i cannot sleep.

true was how my father's love was only

true was how my father's love was only
to my mother
                  most lucky was this love
finding them both in life
                      most lucky me
i am this love
            i am true and only

one had all giving more to the other
one had the other before the world
was enough
           a lifetime was not enough
i am their second lifetime
                    fine and new

fate was tearful yet more joyful
                      thankful
feels everything happened
                      the unhappened
feeling the same for the view on the road
i shall journey on
            still
                my heart is young

My heart is healing

My heart is healing hopefully and Spring
is greening and flowering around me.
I am surrounded by wings of freedom
and wings of self love are growing on me.

Healing from the pain you gave me, my heart
is remembering every Spring in May
and every Fall is forgetting itself.

I am flying and my heart is loving
again like a hope in Spring hopefully.

You gave me pain, darling, my dear darling,
because I let you in my heart truly.
I feel no more pain, because this is Spring,
the first Spring of my new life where birds sing,
understanding the meaning of Spring:
                                        bliss.

Freedom has found me again

179

Freedom has found me again as I knew
it would, whatever the cost of my love
for you was.

       My love for you cost my hate
before it cost my selflessness. I lost
my hopefulness in hopelessness after
my foolishness became my craziness.

My loneliness paid the best price. I am
lonely, nevertheless.

       My love for you
cost as well my love for everything else.
I should have loved everyone else.

       My love
for you has found freedom since lovelessness
found me at the end of this loveless world.

Virus

This is a war between two viruses
(both spreading wide as a disease on earth).
This is, for instance, another crisis
whose final toll will outnumber all deaths.

There is no justice to claim for either,
since this is less than a game for nature.
Do not seek answers from the universe,
since it creates the order in chaos.

Disregarding every meaningful war,
eventually, this must be ended
by the future who ever has a plan
(to history, the present is headed).

This is a war beyond two viruses,
Humana & Corona and what else?
Unless Right & Wrong equal Good & Bad,
still, Yes & No confuse Because & Why.

Migraine

There's a drum in my head and I hear
the rhythm of all that I despise.

In this drumming rhythm, my virtue
&faith etcetera despise me,
because I'm un(able&willing)
to think.

       My life does what my head thinks.

All that is in my head, I despise.
Thus I despise my life, I suppose.

The drum is to blame, making me dumb.

I'm painfully dumb, having a drum
in my head instead of somewhere else
(inside a nuclear bomb, for instance).

no one counts yes two, if three or more

no one counts yes two, if three or more
decent humanbeings and doings
(who make history by unmaking)
think straight on their way to the fall.
both

rightgenocide and leftholocaust
u turn. killing is a mere circle
beginning and ending with itself.

allselves should (by no means
yes, if each number feels numb)give up
ideological idiots,
because dystopia does not need
utopia when the latter needs
the former to make a difference.

remind consciousness of innocence.

On a day, WAR will be over

On a day, WAR will be over,
because every natural thing
& manmade will be.
                           WAR has to
remain everything else, itself
being nothing but how the world
was born to die, living for PEACE.

Until every natural thing
& mankilled will never be again,
there will be forever silence.

On this day, WAR is not over,
because PEACE is loud everywhere.

Let PEACE be patient here & now.

Faith

I have no faith in this world,
therefore (is
a rapee unwillingly fertile)
I have no faith in myself.

It is unimportant,
because (is
a raper wishfully impotent)
little faith is in this world.

Perhaps (is
an asexual sex addict),
I have full faith
in someone in another world.

Sold, freedom sells all else for the price of
death.
          Be brave, let life exploit cowardice
and teach children how to learn from adults.

Not each success or failure does business
(each minding its own) with common nonsense.

Good news is prisons are omnipresent
for worldliness to buy innocence,
the price being forever challenged death.

Bad news is one has to be either rich
or poor in the face of already made
choices.

          Let life be an opportunist,
otherwise, death will refuse to be paid
by freedom.
          Thus, prisons remain legal
when human nature remains natural.

We are more free than we think we are

193

We are more free than we think we are
not slaves.
   Freely, we think, therefore we are.
Freely, freedom is never absolute,
even in thoughts.
   Thus, slaves are what we are.
Freely, nothing is absolute, ever,
even absoluteness.
   Howsoever,
a slave to something, is absolutely
free to itself.
   Freedom is slavery.

Euphoria runs amok

195

Euphoria runs amok wherever
in this immoral yet unlawful world,
satisfaction, almost enough, feels shy
to satisfy an impossible wish.

An orgasm has to learn to be extreme,
despite individual impotence,
if a body has to claim its mind seems
true today, tomorrow being far from truth.

Again, dysphoria digs its own hell
whenever realities see the sun
refuse to shine on every corner. One
sleeps better than two; insomnia fails.

Time&space remain emotionless
when&wherever emotions change.

Everything is now touchable

Everything is now touchable.

                    The sky
is higher than my hands reaching July,
still, I jump high enough to touch August
in its prime.

            Summer touches a goddess
called nature whose beauty belongs to all.
Passion touches burning fires in the air.
I touch the sky and everything is now
in my hands.

             Even the guilt should be proud,
because this is a time for everything
under the sky. Disgraceful is nothing
if it has songs to sing, life understands
(nothing untouchable misunderstands).

Everything I touch is a miracle.
My life is a touchable miracle.

Green

199

Green, greener than the sky dreaming
of blue, bluer than all roses
loving in red, redder than both
white and black painting the same tone
of life and death in four seasons
is breathing in the air.
Timely, nature has the freedom
to be green everywhere.

Greener than gold and silver
coveting silver and gold,
greener than diamonds and pearls
envying pearls and diamonds,
green is the richest color
and the most powerful mode.

Green, greener than prosperity
is the spirit breathing in me.